Slow Cooker Success Cookbook with Easy Instructions for Two

Authentic Recipes With Images & Flavorful Results

By David Clark

Copyright © by David Clark

All rights reserved. This book and its contents are protected under the copyright laws of the United States and other countries. Any unauthorized reproduction, distribution, or transmission of the material within this book, including but not limited to text, graphics, and images, whether in electronic or printed format, is strictly prohibited without the prior written consent of the author, except in the case of brief quotations embodied in critical reviews and scholarly articles.

The recipes, images, and all other content contained in "Slow Cooker Success: Cookbook with Easy Instructions for Two" are the original work of David Clark unless otherwise noted. Each recipe has been authentically created and cooked to ensure originality and authenticity, providing readers with unique culinary experiences.

The publication of this book adheres to the rules and regulations of Kindle Direct Publishing (KDP) concerning copyright standards and content quality. The following features characterize this book:

- It comprises 50 recipes for two people, ensuring intimate and enjoyable dining experiences.
- It is organized into five chapters: Meat, Chicken, Vegetarian, Fish and Seafood, and Soup, each containing 10 authentic recipes.
- Each recipe is accompanied by original, colorful pictures illustrating the expected results, enhancing the user's cooking experience.
- The book is printed in standard color for the paperback version, ensuring high-quality visual appeal.
- Instructions for each recipe are easy to follow, aiming for simplicity in preparation without compromising on the quality of the results.
- All recipes have undergone perfect tests to guarantee perfect flavors, reflecting the author's commitment to culinary excellence.
- The text is meticulously edited to be free of grammatical and spelling errors, maintaining a professional standard throughout the book.

For permissions or inquiries regarding the reproduction and distribution of any material from this book, please get in touch with the author through the publisher. This book is intended for personal use only, and the recipes contained within are meant to provide inspiration and guidance for home cooking.

Introduction

Welcome to the culinary adventure "Slow Cooker Success: Cookbook with Easy Instructions for Two." Crafted with care by David Clark, this collection is more than just a cookbook—it's a gateway to creating unforgettable meals that are as delightful to prepare as they are to share. This book is explicitly designed for pairs, whether couples, roommates, or just two friends who share a love for good food; this book promises to make every meal a memorable experience.

Embark on a journey through the savory world of slow cooking, where each recipe is a discovery of flavors, textures, and aromas. With "Slow Cooker Success," you are not just cooking; you create moments long after the plates are cleared. This book invites you to explore the joys of cooking together, with dishes perfectly portioned for two.

Dive into 50 authentic recipes across five thoughtfully curated chapters: Meat, Chicken, Vegetarian, Fish and Seafood, and Soup. Each chapter offers ten original recipes that have been meticulously tested and perfected, ensuring that you can cook with confidence. From hearty meats to delicate fish and seafood, from vibrant vegetarian dishes to comforting soups, there's something for every palate, every occasion.

Imagine the aromas that will fill your home, the flavors that will tantalize your taste buds and the textures that will delight your senses. Every recipe comes with original, colorful pictures, making the cooking process as visually appealing as it is delicious. The standard color printing of this paperback enhances the visual experience, guiding you through each step with ease and inspiration.

"Slow Cooker Success" is designed to be user-friendly, with easy-to-follow instructions that ensure perfect tests and flavors every time. The meticulous attention to detail extends to the book's quality, which is free from grammatical or spelling errors, allowing you to focus entirely on the joy of cooking and eating.

David Clark invites you to open this book and let the magic of slow cooking transform your meals into something extraordinary. Whether you're looking to spice up your weekday dinners or find the perfect recipe for a special occasion, "Slow Cooker Success: Cookbook with Easy Instructions for Two" is your companion in culinary exploration. Let's begin this delicious journey together.

Table of Contents

Chapter 01: Savory Meat Melodies

Recipe 01: Pot Roast With Vegetables

Savor the rich flavors of this classic slow-cooked pot roast, perfectly combined with carrots, green beans, onions, and garlic, all drenched in a savory gravy. Ideal for a cozy dinner for two, this recipe is a testament to the magic of slow cooking.

Servings: 2

Prepping Time: 15 Minutes

Cook Time: 8 Hours

Difficulty: Easy

Ingredients:

- ✓ 1 lb beef pot roast
- ✓ 2 large carrots, chopped
- ✓ 1 cup green beans, trimmed
- ✓ 1 medium onion, sliced
- ✓ 2 cloves garlic, minced
- ✓ 1 cup beef broth
- ✓ 1 tsp salt
- ✓ 1/2 tsp black pepper
- ✓ 1 tbsp olive oil
- ✓ 2 tbsp flour (for gravy)

Step-by-Step Preparation:

1. Heat olive oil in a pan, brown the pot roast on all sides, and transfer to the slow cooker.
2. In the same pan, sauté onions and garlic until translucent.
3. Place carrots and green beans around the roast in the slow cooker.
4. Add sautéed onions and garlic.
5. Pour beef broth over the ingredients and season with salt and pepper.
6. Cover and cook on low for 8 hours.
7. Remove the roast and vegetables.
8. Use the liquid and flour to make gravy.
9. Serve the roast and vegetables with sauce on top.

Nutritional Facts: (Per serving)

- ❖ Calories: 450
- ❖ Protein: 35g
- ❖ Carbohydrates: 20g
- ❖ Fat: 25g
- ❖ Sodium: 750mg
- ❖ Fiber: 4g

Conclude your day with this heartwarming and filling pot roast, a perfect blend of tender meat and vegetables; all enveloped in a rich, homemade gravy. This dish satisfies your hunger and brings comfort and warmth to your dinner table.

Recipe 02: Pork With Sugar Glazing

Indulge in slow-cooked pork's sweet and savory delight with a luscious sugar glazing. Perfect for a special dinner for two, this dish combines the tenderness of pork with a caramelized, glossy finish, offering a delectable balance of flavors.

Servings: 2

Cook Time: 6 Hours

Prepping Time: 20 Minutes

Difficulty: Moderate

Ingredients:

- ✓ 1 lb pork loin
- ✓ 1/4 cup brown sugar
- ✓ 2 tbsp honey
- ✓ 1 tbsp soy sauce
- ✓ 1 tsp garlic powder
- ✓ 1/2 tsp ground ginger
- ✓ Salt and pepper to taste
- ✓ 1/2 cup water

Step-by-Step Preparation:

1. Mix brown sugar, honey, soy sauce, garlic powder, ginger, salt, and pepper in a small bowl.
2. Place pork loin in the slow cooker and pour the sugar mixture.
3. Add water to the base of the cooker.
4. Cover and cook on low for 6 hours, turning the pork occasionally.
5. Once cooked, remove the pork and let it rest for a few minutes.
6. Slice the pork and drizzle with the glaze from the cooker.

Nutritional Facts: (Per serving)

- ❖ Calories: 510
- ❖ Protein: 40g
- ❖ Carbohydrates: 35g
- ❖ Fat: 20g
- ❖ Sodium: 420mg
- ❖ Sugar: 30g

End your day on a high note with this exquisitely slow-cooked pork, its sugar glazing, creating a perfect harmony of flavors. This dish not only tantalizes your taste buds but also provides a comforting, homely experience, ideal for a quiet, intimate evening.

Recipe 03: Braised Slow Cooked Lamb

Experience the richness of braised slow-cooked lamb shank, bathed in a luxurious red wine sauce, accompanied by shallots and carrots. This dish, perfect for a cozy dinner for two, marries the deep flavors of lamb with the elegance of red wine, creating a gourmet experience at home.

Servings: 2

Cook Time: 7 Hours

Prepping Time: 30 Minutes

Difficulty: Intermediate

Ingredients:

- ✓ 2 lamb shanks
- ✓ 1 cup red wine
- ✓ 2 large carrots, chopped
- ✓ 4 shallots, peeled
- ✓ 2 cloves garlic, minced
- ✓ 1 cup beef broth
- ✓ 2 tbsp olive oil
- ✓ 1 tsp rosemary
- ✓ 1 tsp thyme
- ✓ Salt and pepper to taste

Step-by-Step Preparation:

1. Season lamb shanks with salt, pepper, rosemary, and thyme.
2. Heat olive oil in a pan and brown the lamb shanks on all sides.
3. Transfer the lamb to the slow cooker.
4. In the same pan, sauté shallots and garlic until golden.
5. Add sautéed shallots, garlic, and chopped carrots to the slow cooker.
6. Pour red wine and beef broth over the lamb.
7. Cover and cook on low for 7 hours.
8. Once done, let the lamb rest before serving.
9. Serve with the red wine sauce and vegetables from the cooker.

Nutritional Facts: (Per serving)

- ❖ Calories: 600
- ❖ Protein: 50g
- ❖ Carbohydrates: 15g
- ❖ Fat: 30g
- ❖ Sodium: 500mg
- ❖ Fiber: 3g

Wrap up your evening with this exquisite lamb shank, tenderly cooked to perfection and drenched in a rich red wine sauce. This dish isn't just a meal; it's a celebration of flavors, making your dinner experience both luxurious and deeply satisfying.

Recipe 04: Ribs With Pasta and Grilled Vegetables

Delight in the harmonious blend of slow-cooked ribs, homemade pasta, and grilled vegetables. This dish offers a satisfying mix of tender, flavorful meat, fresh pasta, and the charred goodness of seasonal veggies. Ideal for an intimate dinner for two, it's a culinary journey that combines comfort and sophistication.

Servings: 2

Prepping Time: 45 Minutes

Cook Time: 6 Hours

Difficulty: Advanced

Ingredients:

- ✓ 1 lb pork ribs
- ✓ 1 cup BBQ sauce
- ✓ 1 cup all-purpose flour (for pasta)
- ✓ 2 eggs (for pasta)
- ✓ 1 zucchini, sliced
- ✓ 1 bell pepper, sliced
- ✓ 2 tbsp olive oil (for vegetables)
- ✓ Salt and pepper to taste

Step-by-Step Preparation:

1. Season ribs with salt and pepper, and cover with BBQ sauce in the slow cooker.
2. Cook on low for 6 hours until tender.
3. For pasta, mix flour and eggs to form a dough, knead, and let rest for 30 minutes.
4. Roll out the pasta dough and cut into desired shapes.
5. Boil pasta in salted water until al dente, then drain.
6. Toss zucchini and bell pepper with olive oil, salt, and pepper, and grill until charred.
7. Serve ribs with homemade pasta and grilled vegetables on the side.

Nutritional Facts: (Per serving)

- ❖ Calories: 800
- ❖ Protein: 50g
- ❖ Carbohydrates: 60g
- ❖ Fat: 40g
- ❖ Sodium: 1200mg
- ❖ Fiber: 4g

Conclude your meal with this delightful combination of succulent ribs, fresh pasta, and grilled veggies. It's a dish that fills you up and brings the joy of homemade cooking to your table, perfect for a special evening with your loved one.

Recipe 05: Slow Cooked Pulled Beef

Immerse yourself in the deep, smoky flavors of slow-cooked pulled beef, traditionally rubbed with aromatic spices. This dish, perfect for two, brings the essence of slow smoking to your kitchen, offering tender, flavorful meat that falls apart with every forkful, making it a delightful culinary experience.

Servings: 2

Cook Time: 8 Hours

Prepping Time: 20 Minutes

Difficulty: Medium

Ingredients:

- ✓ 1 lb beef brisket
- ✓ 2 tbsp brown sugar
- ✓ 1 tbsp smoked paprika
- ✓ 1 tsp garlic powder
- ✓ 1 tsp onion powder
- ✓ 1/2 tsp cumin
- ✓ 1/2 tsp chili powder
- ✓ Salt and pepper to taste
- ✓ 1 cup beef broth

Step-by-Step Preparation:

1. Mix brown sugar, smoked paprika, garlic powder, onion powder, cumin, chili powder, salt, and pepper to create the rub.
2. Rub the mixture thoroughly over the brisket.
3. Place the rubbed brisket in the slow cooker.
4. Pour beef broth around the brisket.
5. Cook on low for 8 hours until the beef is tender and easily shreds.
6. Shred the meat with two forks and mix with the cooking juices.

Nutritional Facts: (Per serving)

- ❖ Calories: 550
- ❖ Protein: 60g
- ❖ Carbohydrates: 15g
- ❖ Fat: 25g
- ❖ Sodium: 500mg
- ❖ Fiber: 1g

Complete your meal with this exquisitely tender pulled beef infused with a smoky depth and a medley of spices. It's a hearty, comforting dish that brings the essence of traditional smoking methods to your dining table, perfect for a cozy and satisfying dinner for two.

Recipe 06: Shredded Chicken Breast Stew

Dive into the heartwarming flavors of shredded chicken breast stew, simmered to perfection with a rich tomato sauce, red pepper, onion, and broccoli. This comforting dish is a delightful blend of tender chicken and fresh vegetables, making it an ideal meal for a cozy dinner for two.

Servings: 2

Cook Time: 4 Hours

Prepping Time: 15 Minutes

Difficulty: Easy

Ingredients:

- ✓ 2 chicken breasts
- ✓ 1 cup tomato sauce
- ✓ 1 red bell pepper, sliced
- ✓ 1 onion, chopped
- ✓ 1 cup broccoli florets
- ✓ 1 tsp garlic powder
- ✓ 1 tsp Italian seasoning
- ✓ Salt and pepper to taste
- ✓ 1/2 cup chicken broth

Step-by-Step Preparation:

1. Place chicken breasts in the slow cooker.
2. Add sliced red bell pepper, chopped onion, and broccoli florets.
3. Pour tomato sauce and chicken broth over the ingredients.
4. Season with garlic powder, Italian seasoning, salt, and pepper.
5. Cover and cook on low for 4 hours.
6. Once cooked, shred the chicken in the pot and stir well.

Nutritional Facts: (Per serving)

- ❖ Calories: 310
- ❖ Protein: 35g
- ❖ Carbohydrates: 20g
- ❖ Fat: 8g
- ❖ Sodium: 450mg
- ❖ Fiber: 4g

Wrap up your day with this nourishing and flavorful shredded chicken stew, a perfect balance of protein-rich chicken and vibrant vegetables. It's not just a meal; it's a comforting embrace in a bowl, ideal for winding down and enjoying a peaceful, satisfying dinner.

Recipe 07: Beef Meat Stewed With Potatoes, Carrots and Spices

Delve into the heartwarming comfort of a classic beef stew, slowly cooked with potatoes, carrots, and a symphony of spices. This slow cooker dish is a quintessential comfort food, perfect for a cozy dinner for two. Each spoonful promises a richly flavored and profoundly satisfying blend of tender beef and vegetables.

Servings: 2

Cook Time: 8 Hours

Prepping Time: 20 Minutes

Difficulty: Easy

Ingredients:

- ✓ 1 lb beef stew meat
- ✓ 2 medium potatoes, cubed
- ✓ 2 carrots, sliced
- ✓ 1 onion, diced
- ✓ 2 cloves garlic, minced
- ✓ 1 tsp salt
- ✓ 1/2 tsp black pepper
- ✓ 1 tsp paprika
- ✓ 1/2 tsp dried thyme
- ✓ 2 cups beef broth

Step-by-Step Preparation:

1. Place beef stew meat in the slow cooker.
2. Add cubed potatoes, sliced carrots, and diced onion.
3. Mix in minced garlic, salt, pepper, paprika, and thyme.
4. Pour beef broth over the ingredients, ensuring they are well covered.
5. Cover and cook on low for 8 hours, until the beef is tender and vegetables are soft.
6. Stir the stew and adjust the seasoning as needed before serving.

Nutritional Facts: (Per serving)

- ❖ Calories: 560
- ❖ Protein: 40g
- ❖ Carbohydrates: 45g
- ❖ Fat: 25g
- ❖ Sodium: 950mg
- ❖ Fiber: 6g

Conclude your day with this soul-satisfying beef stew, where each bite reminds you of home-cooked comfort. It's a dish that fills your stomach and warms your heart, making it the perfect end to a cold day or busy week.

Recipe 08: Meat With Mushrooms and Potatoes

Enjoy a cozy evening with this hearty Meat with Mushrooms and Potatoes dish, complemented by grilled tomatoes, zesty herbs, and lemon. Perfect for slow cooking, this recipe for two brings a delightful blend of flavors and aromas to your table.

Servings: 2

Prepping Time: 20 minutes

Cook Time: 6 hours

Difficulty: Medium

Ingredients:

- ✓ 500g beef or pork, cut into chunks
- ✓ 200g mushrooms, sliced
- ✓ 2 large potatoes, cubed
- ✓ 2 tomatoes, halved
- ✓ 1 lemon, zested and juiced
- ✓ 2 cloves garlic, minced
- ✓ 1 tbsp fresh rosemary, chopped
- ✓ 1 tbsp fresh thyme, chopped
- ✓ Salt and pepper, to taste
- ✓ 2 tbsp olive oil

Step-by-Step Preparation:

1. Season the meat with salt, pepper, and half lemon zest.
2. In the slow cooker, layer potatoes, mushrooms, and seasoned beef.
3. Mix lemon juice, garlic, rosemary, thyme, and olive oil. Pour over the meat mixture.
4. Cook on low for 6 hours until meat is tender.
5. In the last 30 minutes, add grilled tomatoes on top.
6. Garnish with remaining lemon zest and herbs before serving.

Nutritional Facts: (Per serving)

- ❖ Calories: 650
- ❖ Protein: 35g
- ❖ Carbohydrates: 45g
- ❖ Fat: 35g
- ❖ Fiber: 6g
- ❖ Sodium: 300mg

Conclude your day with this comforting and flavorful dish. It's the perfect way to enjoy a relaxed, slow-cooked meal that combines the earthy goodness of mushrooms and potatoes with the vibrant zest of lemon and herbs.

Recipe 09: Irish Beef Stew With Carrots and Potatoes

Savor the warmth and comfort of a traditional Irish Beef Stew, richly flavored with carrots and potatoes. This slow cooker recipe is perfect for two, offering a taste of Ireland in every spoonful.

Servings: 2

Cook Time: 8 hours

Prepping Time: 15 minutes

Difficulty: Easy

Ingredients:

- ✓ 300g beef stew meat, cubed
- ✓ 2 large carrots, sliced
- ✓ 2 medium potatoes, cubed
- ✓ 1 onion, chopped
- ✓ 2 cloves garlic, minced
- ✓ 2 cups beef broth
- ✓ 1 tbsp tomato paste
- ✓ 1 tsp dried thyme
- ✓ Salt and pepper, to taste
- ✓ 2 tbsp olive oil

Step-by-Step Preparation:

1. In a pan, brown the beef cubes in olive oil. Transfer to the slow cooker.
2. Add carrots, potatoes, onion, and garlic to the slow cooker.
3. Mix beef broth, tomato paste, thyme, salt, and pepper. Pour over the ingredients in the slow cooker.
4. Set the slow cooker to low and cook for 8 hours until the beef is tender.
5. Adjust seasoning as needed before serving.

Nutritional Facts: (Per serving)

- ❖ Calories: 520
- ❖ Protein: 36g
- ❖ Carbohydrates: 45g
- ❖ Fat: 22g
- ❖ Fiber: 6g
- ❖ Sodium: 480mg

Enjoy the heartwarming flavors of this Irish Beef Stew. Its slow-cooked tenderness and rich blend of carrots and potatoes make it an ideal comfort dish for a cozy night in.

Recipe 10: Meat Stew With Beef

Indulge in the hearty and comforting flavors of a classic Meat Stew featuring tender beef, potatoes, carrots, onions, spices, and green peas. This slow cooker recipe serves two, offering a wholesome and satisfying meal perfect for any day of the week.

Servings: 2

Cook Time: 7 hours

Prepping Time: 20 minutes

Difficulty: Easy

Ingredients:

- ✓ 300g beef stew meat, cubed
- ✓ 1 large potato, cubed
- ✓ 1 carrot, sliced
- ✓ 1 onion, chopped
- ✓ 1 cup green peas
- ✓ 2 cloves garlic, minced
- ✓ 2 cups beef broth
- ✓ 1 tsp paprika
- ✓ 1 tsp dried thyme
- ✓ Salt and pepper, to taste
- ✓ 2 tbsp olive oil

Step-by-Step Preparation:

1. Brown the beef cubes in olive oil and transfer to the slow cooker.
2. Add potato, carrot, onion, and garlic to the beef in the cooker.
3. Pour beef broth over the mixture and add paprika, thyme, salt, and pepper.
4. Cook on low for 6 hours.
5. Stir in green peas and cook for an additional hour.
6. Adjust seasoning if needed before serving.

Nutritional Facts: (Per serving)

- ❖ Calories: 550
- ❖ Protein: 40g
- ❖ Carbohydrates: 45g
- ❖ Fat: 25g
- ❖ Fiber: 7g
- ❖ Sodium: 500mg

Relish this delicious meat stew with beef, vegetables, and a spice blend. It's a simple yet fulfilling dish perfect for a relaxing evening or a weekend dinner.

Chapter 02: Tender Chicken Delights

Recipe 11: Chicken Taco Soup

Experience the zesty and vibrant flavors of Chicken Taco Soup, a delightful dish infused with a blend of spices and topped with fresh cilantro. This slow cooker recipe is an easy and flavorful way to enjoy a Mexican-inspired meal for two.

Servings: 2

Prepping Time: 15 minutes

Cook Time: 6 hours

Difficulty: Easy

Ingredients:

- ✓ 300g chicken breast, cubed
- ✓ 1 can diced tomatoes
- ✓ 1 can black beans, drained
- ✓ 1 cup corn kernels
- ✓ 1 onion, chopped
- ✓ 2 cloves garlic, minced
- ✓ 1 tbsp taco seasoning
- ✓ 2 cups chicken broth
- ✓ Salt and pepper, to taste
- ✓ Fresh cilantro for garnish

Step-by-Step Preparation:

1. Place chicken, diced tomatoes, black beans, corn, onion, and garlic in the slow cooker.
2. Season with taco seasoning, salt, and pepper.
3. Pour chicken broth over the mixture and stir well.
4. Cook on low for 6 hours until chicken is tender.
5. Shred the chicken in the soup, if desired.
6. Serve hot, garnished with fresh cilantro.

Nutritional Facts: (Per serving)

- ❖ Calories: 400
- ❖ Protein: 35g
- ❖ Carbohydrates: 50g
- ❖ Fat: 10g
- ❖ Fiber: 10g
- ❖ Sodium: 700mg

After a long day, unwind with this comforting bowl of Chicken Taco Soup. Its rich flavors and fresh cilantro topping make it a delightful and easy meal that's sure to please.

Recipe 12: White Chili Chicken With Beans and Corn

Dive into the creamy and savory world of White Chili Chicken, a delightful slow cooker dish that combines tender chicken with beans and corn for a comforting meal. This recipe for two is easy to make and full of flavor, ideal for a cozy night in.

Servings: 2

Prepping Time: 15 minutes

Cook Time: 6 hours

Difficulty: Easy

Ingredients:

- ✓ 300g boneless chicken breast
- ✓ 1 can white beans, drained
- ✓ 1 cup corn kernels
- ✓ 1 onion, chopped
- ✓ 2 cloves garlic, minced
- ✓ 1 tsp cumin
- ✓ 1 tsp chili powder
- ✓ 2 cups chicken broth
- ✓ Salt and pepper, to taste
- ✓ Sour cream and fresh cilantro for garnish

Step-by-Step Preparation:

1. Place chicken, white beans, corn, onion, and garlic in the slow cooker.
2. Season with cumin, chili powder, salt, and pepper.
3. Pour chicken broth over the ingredients.
4. Cook on low for 6 hours until chicken is tender.
5. Shred the chicken in the cooker and stir well.
6. Serve with a dollop of sour cream and a sprinkle of fresh cilantro.

Nutritional Facts: (Per serving)

- ❖ Calories: 420
- ❖ Protein: 38g
- ❖ Carbohydrates: 50g
- ❖ Fat: 10g
- ❖ Fiber: 8g
- ❖ Sodium: 690mg

Conclude your day with this hearty and nourishing White Chili Chicken. It's the perfect blend of simplicity and taste, offering a comforting meal to warm your heart and satisfy your taste buds.

Recipe 13: Chicken Vegetable Stew

Indulge in the wholesome goodness of Chicken Vegetable Stew, a nutritious and flavorful slow cooker dish perfect for two. Packed with tender chicken and fresh vegetables, this stew is a comforting and easy-to-make meal, ideal for busy evenings or a relaxed weekend dinner.

Servings: 2

Prepping Time: 20 minutes

Cook Time: 6 hours

Difficulty: Easy

Ingredients:

- ✓ 300g chicken breast, cubed
- ✓ 1 carrot, sliced
- ✓ 1 potato, cubed
- ✓ 1 onion, chopped
- ✓ 1 cup green beans, trimmed
- ✓ 2 cloves garlic, minced
- ✓ 2 cups chicken broth
- ✓ 1 tsp dried thyme
- ✓ Salt and pepper, to taste

Step-by-Step Preparation:

1. Place the chicken, carrot, potato, onion, and green beans in the slow cooker.
2. Add minced garlic, thyme, salt, and pepper.
3. Pour chicken broth over the vegetables and chicken.
4. Cook on low for 6 hours until the chicken is tender and the vegetables are cooked.
5. Adjust seasoning if needed before serving.

Nutritional Facts: (Per serving)

- ❖ Calories: 380
- ❖ Protein: 38g
- ❖ Carbohydrates: 35g
- ❖ Fat: 10g
- ❖ Fiber: 5g
- ❖ Sodium: 450mg

Wrap up your day with this comforting Chicken Vegetable Stew. Its rich flavors and hearty ingredients make it an ideal dish to savor, providing both nutrition and taste in each spoonful.

Recipe 14: Chicken Stew With Potatoes and Vegetables

Discover the heartwarming flavors of Chicken Stew with Potatoes and Vegetables, a slow cooker recipe perfect for two. This dish combines succulent chicken, hearty potatoes, and a medley of vegetables simmered to perfection, creating a comforting and nutritious meal ideal for any day of the week.

Servings: 2

Cook Time: 6 hours

Prepping Time: 20 minutes

Difficulty: Easy

Ingredients:

- ✓ 300g chicken breast, cubed
- ✓ 2 medium potatoes, cubed
- ✓ 1 carrot, sliced
- ✓ 1 bell pepper, chopped
- ✓ 1 onion, chopped
- ✓ 2 cloves garlic, minced
- ✓ 2 cups chicken broth
- ✓ 1 tsp dried oregano
- ✓ Salt and pepper, to taste

Step-by-Step Preparation:

1. Place chicken, potatoes, carrots, bell pepper, and onion in the slow cooker.
2. Add garlic, oregano, salt, and pepper.
3. Pour chicken broth over the mixture.
4. Cook on low for 6 hours until chicken and vegetables are tender.
5. Stir well and adjust seasoning as needed before serving.

Nutritional Facts: (Per serving)

- ❖ Calories: 400
- ❖ Protein: 38g
- ❖ Carbohydrates: 40g
- ❖ Fat: 12g
- ❖ Fiber: 6g
- ❖ Sodium: 480mg

End your day with this comforting Chicken Stew, a delightful blend of flavors and textures. It's a simple yet satisfying meal that's sure to become a favorite for its ease of preparation and wholesome taste.

Recipe 15: Shredded Chicken Breast Stew

Embark on a flavorful journey with this shredded chicken breast stew, a slow cooker delight featuring a rich tomato sauce, red pepper, onion, and broccoli. Perfect for two, this dish offers a blend of savory and hearty elements, making it an ideal choice for a comforting and nutritious meal any day of the week.

Servings: 2

Cook Time: 5 hours

Prepping Time: 15 minutes

Difficulty: Easy

Ingredients:

- ✓ 300g chicken breast
- ✓ 1 cup tomato sauce
- ✓ 1 red pepper, chopped
- ✓ 1 onion, chopped
- ✓ 1 cup broccoli florets
- ✓ 2 cloves garlic, minced
- ✓ 1 tsp dried basil
- ✓ Salt and pepper, to taste

Step-by-Step Preparation:

1. Place chicken breast in the slow cooker.
2. Add tomato sauce, red pepper, onion, and garlic.
3. Season with basil, salt, and pepper.
4. Cook on low for 5 hours until chicken is tender.
5. Shred the chicken in the cooker, then add broccoli florets.
6. Cook for an additional 30 minutes.
7. Stir well before serving.

Nutritional Facts: (Per serving)

- ❖ Calories: 350
- ❖ Protein: 40g
- ❖ Carbohydrates: 25g
- ❖ Fat: 10g
- ❖ Fiber: 5g
- ❖ Sodium: 400mg

Enjoy this delectable shredded chicken breast stew, a perfect combination of protein-packed chicken and vibrant vegetables in a luscious tomato sauce. It's a wonderfully easy and satisfying meal that brings comfort and nutrition to your table with minimal effort.

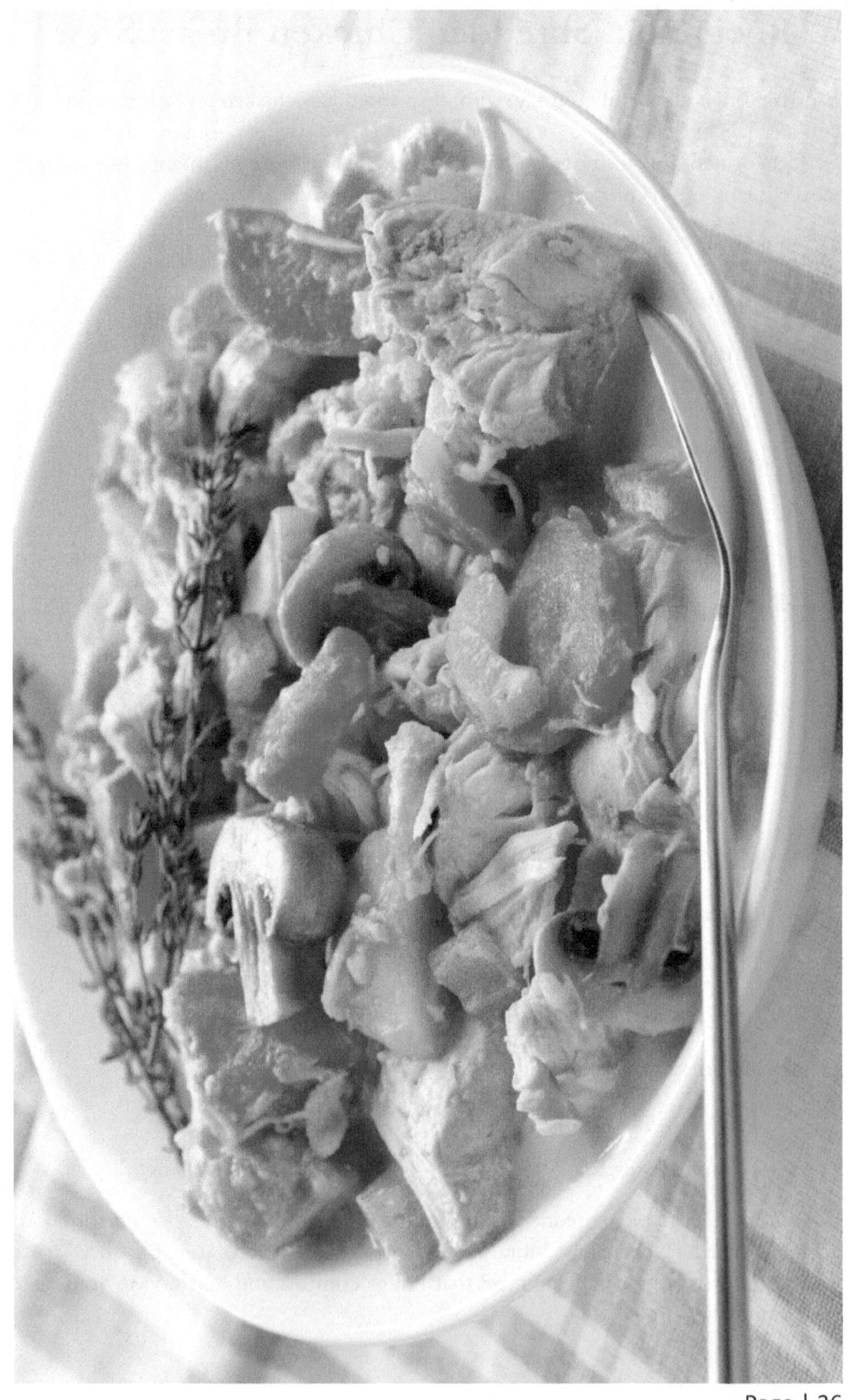

Recipe 16: Chicken Stew With Herbs

Delight in the rich and creamy flavors of this Chicken Stew, a slow cooker masterpiece that combines tender chicken with a medley of vegetables, earthy mushrooms, and fragrant herbs, all in a creamy sauce. It's a perfect, comforting meal for two, ideal for a cozy night.

Servings: 2

Cook Time: 5 hours

Prepping Time: 20 minutes

Difficulty: Medium

Ingredients:

- ✓ 300g chicken breast, cubed
- ✓ 1 cup mushrooms, sliced
- ✓ 1 carrot, sliced
- ✓ 1 potato, cubed
- ✓ 1 onion, chopped
- ✓ 2 cloves garlic, minced
- ✓ 1 cup chicken broth
- ✓ ½ cup heavy cream
- ✓ 1 tsp dried thyme
- ✓ 1 tsp dried rosemary
- ✓ Salt and pepper, to taste

Step-by-Step Preparation:

1. Place chicken, mushrooms, carrot, potato, and onion in the slow cooker.
2. Add garlic, thyme, rosemary, salt, and pepper.
3. Pour chicken broth over the ingredients.
4. Cook on low for 4 hours until chicken is tender.
5. Stir in heavy cream and cook for 1 more hour.
6. Adjust seasoning if necessary before serving.

Nutritional Facts: (Per serving)

- ❖ Calories: 450
- ❖ Protein: 38g
- ❖ Carbohydrates: 35g
- ❖ Fat: 20g
- ❖ Fiber: 4g
- ❖ Sodium: 450mg

This Chicken Stew is a symphony of flavors and textures, making every bite a delightful experience. It's the perfect dish to savor when you crave something hearty, creamy, and utterly satisfying.

Recipe 17: Chicken Cacciatore With Tender Chicken Breasts

Embark on a culinary adventure with Chicken Cacciatore, a classic Italian dish reimagined for the slow cooker. This recipe features tender chicken breasts simmered with tomatoes, bell peppers, carrots, and sliced mushrooms, creating a rich and satisfying meal perfect for two. It's an effortless way to bring the flavors of Italy to your dinner table.

Servings: 2

Cook Time: 6 hours

Prepping Time: 20 minutes

Difficulty: Easy

Ingredients:

- ✓ 2 chicken breasts
- ✓ 1 can diced tomatoes
- ✓ 1 bell pepper, sliced
- ✓ 2 carrots, sliced
- ✓ 1 cup mushrooms, sliced
- ✓ 1 onion, chopped
- ✓ 2 cloves garlic, minced
- ✓ 1 tsp dried oregano
- ✓ Salt and pepper, to taste

Step-by-Step Preparation:

1. Place chicken breasts in the slow cooker.
2. Add diced tomatoes, bell pepper, carrots, mushrooms, onion, and garlic.
3. Season with oregano, salt, and pepper.
4. Cook on low for 6 hours until chicken is tender and vegetables are cooked.
5. Break the chicken into smaller pieces, if desired, and stir well.
6. Adjust seasoning before serving.

Nutritional Facts: (Per serving)

- ❖ Calories: 350
- ❖ Protein: 35g
- ❖ Carbohydrates: 30g
- ❖ Fat: 10g
- ❖ Fiber: 6g
- ❖ Sodium: 400mg

Conclude your day with this delightful Chicken cacciatore, a dish combining simplicity and rich, comforting flavors. It's a perfect meal for those who love the essence of Italian cooking with the ease of a slow cooker.

Recipe 18: Golden Brown Pork Belly

Indulge in the rich and savory taste of golden brown pork belly slices, slow-cooked to perfection, in a flavorful brown sauce. Although labeled as a chicken recipe, this dish is a delightful twist that offers a tender and juicy pork experience for two, making it an ideal choice for a unique yet easy home-cooked meal.

Servings: 2

Cook Time: 6 hours

Prepping Time: 15 minutes

Difficulty: Easy

Ingredients:

- ✓ 500g pork belly, sliced
- ✓ 1 cup brown sauce
- ✓ 1 onion, chopped
- ✓ 2 cloves garlic, minced
- ✓ 1 tbsp soy sauce
- ✓ 1 tsp honey
- ✓ Salt and pepper, to taste

Step-by-Step Preparation:

1. Place pork belly slices in the slow cooker.
2. Combine brown sauce, onion, garlic, soy sauce, honey, salt, and pepper in a bowl.
3. Pour the sauce mixture over the pork belly.
4. Cook on low for 6 hours until the pork is tender and golden brown.
5. Occasionally, baste the pork with the sauce during cooking.

Nutritional Facts: (Per serving)

- ❖ Calories: 650
- ❖ Protein: 30g
- ❖ Carbohydrates: 15g
- ❖ Fat: 50g
- ❖ Fiber: 1g
- ❖ Sodium: 700mg

After a long day, enjoy these succulent pork belly slices, richly flavored and beautifully tender. It's a luxurious yet simple dish, perfect for those evenings when you crave something satisfying.

Recipe 19: Chicken Thigh Fricassee Stew

Embark on a culinary journey to Britain with this Chicken Thigh Fricassee Stew. This delightful slow cooker dish combines tender chicken thighs with colorful vegetables in a creamy white sauce. Perfect for two, this recipe brings a touch of British elegance to your dinner table, offering a comforting and hearty meal.

Servings: 2

Prepping Time: 20 minutes

Cook Time: 5 hours

Difficulty: Medium

Ingredients:

- ✓ 4 chicken thighs, boneless and skinless
- ✓ 1 cup mixed vegetables (carrots, peas, bell peppers)
- ✓ 1 onion, chopped
- ✓ 2 cloves garlic, minced
- ✓ 2 cups chicken broth
- ✓ ½ cup heavy cream
- ✓ 2 tbsp flour
- ✓ 1 tsp dried thyme
- ✓ Salt and pepper, to taste

Step-by-Step Preparation:

1. Place chicken thighs in the slow cooker.
2. Add mixed vegetables, onion, and garlic.
3. Whisk together chicken broth, heavy cream, flour, thyme, salt, and pepper in a bowl. Pour over the chicken and vegetables.
4. Cook on low for 5 hours until the chicken is tender and the sauce thickens.
5. Stir gently to combine before serving.

Nutritional Facts: (Per serving)

- ❖ Calories: 450
- ❖ Protein: 30g
- ❖ Carbohydrates: 20g
- ❖ Fat: 25g
- ❖ Fiber: 3g
- ❖ Sodium: 450mg

Finish your day with this exquisite British Chicken Thigh Fricassee Stew. Its creamy sauce and tender chicken, accompanied by vibrant vegetables, create a symphony of both comforting and satisfying flavors, perfect for a cozy night in.

Recipe 20: Chicken Tajine

Embark on a culinary adventure with Chicken Tajine, a Moroccan slow-cooked dish that brings the exotic flavors of North Africa to your table. This recipe, perfect for two, combines tender chicken with aromatic spices and slow-cooked perfection, creating a meal that's not only delicious but also deeply rooted in Moroccan culinary traditions.

Servings: 2

Cook Time: 6 hours

Prepping Time: 15 minutes

Difficulty: Medium

Ingredients:

- ✓ 2 chicken thighs
- ✓ 1 onion, sliced
- ✓ 2 cloves garlic, minced
- ✓ 1 carrot, sliced
- ✓ 1 cup chickpeas, drained
- ✓ 1 cup diced tomatoes
- ✓ 1 tsp cumin
- ✓ 1 tsp paprika
- ✓ 1/2 tsp cinnamon
- ✓ Salt and pepper, to taste
- ✓ 2 tbsp olive oil
- ✓ Fresh cilantro for garnish

Step-by-Step Preparation:

1. Heat olive oil in a pan and brown chicken thighs. Transfer to the slow cooker.
2. Add onion, garlic, carrot, chickpeas, and diced tomatoes to the cooker.
3. Season with cumin, paprika, cinnamon, salt, and pepper.
4. Cook on low for 6 hours until the chicken is tender.
5. Garnish with fresh cilantro before serving.

Nutritional Facts: (Per serving)

- ❖ Calories: 450
- ❖ Protein: 30g
- ❖ Carbohydrates: 35g
- ❖ Fat: 20g
- ❖ Fiber: 7g
- ❖ Sodium: 300mg

Conclude your day with this flavorful Chicken Tajine, a dish that encapsulates the essence of Moroccan cuisine. Its blend of spices and slow-cooked tenderness is a taste treat, perfect for a special dinner for two.

Chapter 03: Verdant Vegetarian Feasts

Recipe 21: Mushroom and Potato Stew

Embark on a delightful vegetarian journey with this Mushroom and Potato Stew, enhanced with the fresh flavor of green dill. This slow cooker recipe is perfect for two, offering a comforting, heartwarming, simple, and deliciously satisfying meal with earthy mushrooms and tender potatoes seasoned to perfection.

Servings: 2

Prepping Time: 15 minutes

Cook Time: 5 hours

Difficulty: Easy

Ingredients:

- ✓ 2 cups mushrooms, sliced
- ✓ 2 large potatoes, cubed
- ✓ 1 onion, chopped
- ✓ 2 cloves garlic, minced
- ✓ 2 cups vegetable broth
- ✓ 1 tsp dried dill
- ✓ Salt and pepper, to taste
- ✓ 1 tbsp olive oil

Step-by-Step Preparation:

1. Place mushrooms, potatoes, onion, and garlic in the slow cooker.
2. Drizzle with olive oil and season with dill, salt, and pepper.
3. Pour vegetable broth over the ingredients.
4. Cook on low for 5 hours until potatoes are tender and flavors meld.
5. Stir gently before serving.

Nutritional Facts: (Per serving)

- ❖ Calories: 300
- ❖ Protein: 8g
- ❖ Carbohydrates: 50g
- ❖ Fat: 8g
- ❖ Fiber: 6g
- ❖ Sodium: 300mg

End your day with this soul-soothing Vegetarian Mushroom and Potato Stew, where the subtle flavors of dill perfectly complement the earthy mushrooms and hearty potatoes. It's a simple yet fulfilling dish that brings comfort and warmth to any vegetarian table.

Recipe 22: Lebanese Vegetarian Eggplant Stew

Immerse yourself in the flavors of the Middle East with Maghmour, a Lebanese vegetarian eggplant stew. This slow cooker rendition is enriched with chickpeas and is ideally served with warm pita bread. Perfect for two, Maghmour is not just a meal but a celebration of rich, aromatic flavors that embody the essence of Lebanese cuisine.

Servings: 2

Prepping Time: 20 minutes

Cook Time: 4 hours

Difficulty: Easy

Ingredients:

- ✓ 2 medium eggplants, cubed
- ✓ 1 can chickpeas, drained
- ✓ 1 onion, chopped
- ✓ 2 cloves garlic, minced
- ✓ 1 can diced tomatoes
- ✓ 1 tsp cumin
- ✓ 1 tsp paprika
- ✓ Salt and pepper, to taste
- ✓ 2 tbsp olive oil
- ✓ Fresh parsley for garnish
- ✓ Pita bread for serving

Step-by-Step Preparation:

1. Sauté eggplants in olive oil until lightly browned, then transfer to the slow cooker.
2. Add chickpeas, onion, garlic, and diced tomatoes to the cooker.
3. Season with cumin, paprika, salt, and pepper.
4. Cook on low for 4 hours until eggplants are tender.
5. Garnish with fresh parsley and serve with pita bread.

Nutritional Facts: (Per serving)

- ❖ Calories: 380
- ❖ Protein: 12g
- ❖ Carbohydrates: 50g
- ❖ Fat: 18g
- ❖ Fiber: 14g
- ❖ Sodium: 300mg

Conclude your day with this flavorful Lebanese Maghmour, a dish that brings the essence of Middle Eastern vegetarian cuisine to your table. It's a perfect blend of simplicity, health, and taste, ideal for a cozy and cultural dining experience.

Recipe 23: Butternut Squash Scooped From Its Husk

Delve into the sweet and savory world of Butternut Squash, scooped right from its husk, in this simple yet elegant slow cooker dish. Perfect for two, this recipe highlights the natural, rich flavors of butternut squash, making it an ideal vegetarian meal for a cozy night in or a sophisticated dinner.

Servings: 2

Prepping Time: 10 minutes

Cook Time: 4 hours

Difficulty: Easy

Ingredients:

- ✓ 1 large butternut squash
- ✓ 2 tbsp olive oil
- ✓ Salt and pepper, to taste
- ✓ 1 tsp cinnamon
- ✓ 1 tbsp maple syrup
- ✓ Fresh herbs (thyme or sage) for garnish

Step-by-Step Preparation:

1. Cut the butternut squash in half and remove the seeds.
2. Drizzle each half with olive oil, and season with salt, pepper, and cinnamon.
3. Place the squash halves in the slow cooker.
4. Cook on low for 4 hours until the squash is tender.
5. Drizzle with maple syrup and garnish with fresh herbs before serving.

Nutritional Facts: (Per serving)

- ❖ Calories: 240
- ❖ Protein: 2g
- ❖ Carbohydrates: 35g
- ❖ Fat: 12g
- ❖ Fiber: 6g
- ❖ Sodium: 10mg

This Butternut Squash dish is a feast for the taste buds and a visual delight. Enjoy the simplicity and elegance it brings to your dining experience; it is perfect for those who appreciate this versatile vegetable's natural sweetness and richness.

Recipe 24: Escalivada Smoky Slow Roasted Vegetables

Savor the rustic charm of Escalivada, a smoky slow-roasted vegetable dish that hails from the heart of Mediterranean cuisine. This vegetarian recipe for two, featuring a harmonious blend of peppers, eggplant, and onion, celebrates simplicity and flavor, all achieved effortlessly in your slow cooker.

Servings: 2

Cook Time: 5 hours

Prepping Time: 15 minutes

Difficulty: Easy

Ingredients:

- ✓ 1 red bell pepper
- ✓ 1 eggplant
- ✓ 1 large onion
- ✓ 2 tbsp olive oil
- ✓ Salt and pepper, to taste
- ✓ 1 tsp smoked paprika
- ✓ Fresh parsley for garnish

Step-by-Step Preparation:

1. Slice the bell pepper, eggplant, and onion into large chunks.
2. Toss the vegetables with olive oil, salt, pepper, and smoked paprika.
3. Place the seasoned vegetables in the slow cooker.
4. Cook on low for 5 hours until the vegetables are tender and infused with a smoky flavor.
5. Garnish with fresh parsley before serving.

Nutritional Facts: (Per serving)

- ❖ Calories: 180
- ❖ Protein: 3g
- ❖ Carbohydrates: 25g
- ❖ Fat: 10g
- ❖ Fiber: 7g
- ❖ Sodium: 10mg

Finish your day with this delightful Escalivada, where the smokiness of the slow-roasted vegetables creates a symphony of flavors. It's a dish that not only tantalizes the taste buds but also brings the essence of Mediterranean cuisine to your table.

Recipe 25: Vegetarian Mushroom Stuffed Peppers

Immerse yourself in the delightful flavors of Vegetarian Mushroom Stuffed Peppers, a dish that combines the earthiness of mushrooms with the sweetness of bell peppers. This slow cooker recipe, perfect for two, offers a delicious and nutritious vegetarian option that's both easy to prepare and satisfyingly hearty.

Servings: 2

Cook Time: 4 hours

Prepping Time: 20 minutes

Difficulty: Medium

Ingredients:

- ✓ 2 large bell peppers
- ✓ 1 cup mushrooms, finely chopped
- ✓ 1 onion, diced
- ✓ 2 cloves garlic, minced
- ✓ 1/2 cup cooked rice
- ✓ 1/4 cup grated cheese (optional)
- ✓ 1 tsp dried oregano
- ✓ Salt and pepper, to taste
- ✓ 1 tbsp olive oil

Step-by-Step Preparation:

1. Cut the tops off the bell peppers and remove the seeds.
2. In a skillet, sauté mushrooms, onion, and garlic in olive oil until soft.
3. Mix in cooked rice, oregano, salt, and pepper.
4. Stuff this mixture into the bell peppers and top with cheese.
5. Place the stuffed peppers in the slow cooker.
6. Cook on low for 4 hours until peppers are tender.

Nutritional Facts: (Per serving)

- ❖ Calories: 220
- ❖ Protein: 6g
- ❖ Carbohydrates: 28g
- ❖ Fat: 10g
- ❖ Fiber: 5g
- ❖ Sodium: 100mg

Enjoy the perfect blend of flavors and textures in these Vegetarian Mushroom Stuffed Peppers. This dish brings comfort and a touch of gourmet to your everyday meals, making it a delightful option for a cozy and healthy dinner.

Recipe 26: Lobio Slow-Cooked Beans Stew

Embark on a culinary journey to the heart of Georgia with Lobio, a traditional slow-cooked bean stew. Paired with the rustic charm of McHadi, a Georgian cornbread, this vegetarian recipe for two brings a taste of the Caucasus to your table, offering a hearty and flavorful experience that's both nourishing and comforting.

Servings: 2

Cook Time: 8 hours

Prepping Time: 20 minutes

Difficulty: Easy

Ingredients:

- ✓ 1 cup dried red beans, soaked overnight
- ✓ 1 onion, chopped
- ✓ 2 cloves garlic, minced
- ✓ 1 tsp coriander powder
- ✓ 1/2 tsp cumin
- ✓ Salt and pepper, to taste
- ✓ 2 tbsp olive oil
- ✓ Fresh cilantro for garnish
- ✓ McHadi Georgian Cornbread (for serving)

Step-by-Step Preparation:

1. Rinse and drain the soaked beans.
2. Place beans, onion, and garlic in the slow cooker.
3. Season with coriander, cumin, salt, and pepper.
4. Add enough water to cover the beans and drizzle with olive oil.
5. Cook on low for 8 hours until beans are tender.
6. Mash some of the beans for a thicker stew, if desired.
7. Garnish with fresh cilantro and serve with McHadi cornbread.

Nutritional Facts: (Per serving)

- ❖ Calories: 380
- ❖ Protein: 20g
- ❖ Carbohydrates: 55g
- ❖ Fat: 10g
- ❖ Fiber: 15g
- ❖ Sodium: 20mg

Conclude your day with this heartwarming Lobio, a dish that satisfies your hunger and takes you on a flavorful journey through Georgian cuisine. Paired with McHadi cornbread, it's a perfect combination of taste and tradition, ideal for a cozy and fulfilling meal.

Recipe 27: Beans Chili / Vegetarian Chili

Dive into Beans Chili's bold and hearty flavors, a vegetarian delight sure to satisfy. This slow cooker recipe, perfect for two, combines various beans and rich spices, creating a comforting and robust dish. It's an ideal meat-free meal without skimping on flavor or heartiness.

Servings: 2

Prepping Time: 15 minutes

Cook Time: 6 hours

Difficulty: Easy

Ingredients:

- ✓ 1 can of kidney beans, drained
- ✓ 1 can black beans, drained
- ✓ 1 can diced tomatoes
- ✓ 1 onion, chopped
- ✓ 2 cloves garlic, minced
- ✓ 1 green bell pepper, chopped
- ✓ 1 tbsp chili powder
- ✓ 1 tsp cumin
- ✓ Salt and pepper, to taste
- ✓ 1 cup vegetable broth

Step-by-Step Preparation:

1. Combine kidney beans, black beans, diced tomatoes, onion, garlic, and bell pepper in the slow cooker.
2. Season with chili powder, cumin, salt, and pepper.
3. Pour vegetable broth over the mixture.
4. Cook on low for 6 hours, allowing flavors to meld and beans to become tender.
5. Adjust seasoning as needed before serving.

Nutritional Facts: (Per serving)

- ❖ Calories: 330
- ❖ Protein: 18g
- ❖ Carbohydrates: 60g
- ❖ Fat: 3g
- ❖ Fiber: 20g
- ❖ Sodium: 500mg

Wrap up your day with this nourishing and flavorful bean chili, a dish that brings warmth and comfort to any table. Its rich blend of beans and spices makes it a fulfilling and healthy choice for a vegetarian meal.

Recipe 28: Vegetarian Minestrone

Savor the classic Italian flavors with Vegetarian Minestrone, a slow cooker delight perfect for a cozy meal for two. This nutritious and hearty soup combines various fresh vegetables and beans simmered to perfection, offering a comforting and satisfying experience with every spoonful.

Servings: 2

Cook Time: 6 hours

Prepping Time: 15 minutes

Difficulty: Easy

Ingredients:

- ✓ 1 can diced tomatoes
- ✓ 1 carrot, chopped
- ✓ 1 celery stalk, chopped
- ✓ 1 onion, chopped
- ✓ 1 zucchini, chopped
- ✓ 1 cup spinach, chopped
- ✓ 1 can of kidney beans, drained
- ✓ 3 cups vegetable broth
- ✓ 1 tsp dried basil
- ✓ 1 tsp dried oregano
- ✓ Salt and pepper, to taste

Step-by-Step Preparation:

1. Place diced tomatoes, carrots, celery, onion, and zucchini in the slow cooker.
2. Add kidney beans and spinach.
3. Season with basil, oregano, salt, and pepper.
4. Pour vegetable broth over the vegetables.
5. Cook on low for 6 hours until vegetables are tender.
6. Adjust seasoning as needed before serving.

Nutritional Facts: (Per serving)

- ❖ Calories: 250
- ❖ Protein: 12g
- ❖ Carbohydrates: 45g
- ❖ Fat: 2g
- ❖ Fiber: 12g
- ❖ Sodium: 300mg

End your day with this delightful Vegetarian Minestrone, a soup that warms your body and soul. It's a wholesome, nourishing dish that celebrates the simplicity and richness of Italian cooking, perfect for a relaxing and healthy meal.

Recipe 29: Moroccan Tagine With Rice

Experience the exotic flavors of Morocco with this Vegetarian Moroccan Tagine, a slow cooker dish perfect for two. Combining aromatic spices and a variety of vegetables, this tagine is served with fluffy rice, creating a meal that's both culturally rich and delightfully flavorful, ideal for an adventurous yet comforting dining experience.

Servings: 2

Cook Time: 6 hours

Prepping Time: 20 minutes

Difficulty: Medium

Ingredients:

- ✓ 1 cup diced tomatoes
- ✓ 1 carrot, sliced
- ✓ 1 zucchini, sliced
- ✓ 1 bell pepper, chopped
- ✓ 1 onion, chopped
- ✓ 2 cloves garlic, minced
- ✓ 1 tsp cumin
- ✓ 1 tsp paprika
- ✓ 1/2 tsp cinnamon
- ✓ Salt and pepper, to taste
- ✓ 1 cup vegetable broth
- ✓ 1 cup cooked rice for serving

Step-by-Step Preparation:

1. Place tomatoes, carrots, zucchini, bell pepper, onion, and garlic in the slow cooker.
2. Season with cumin, paprika, cinnamon, salt, and pepper.
3. Pour vegetable broth over the vegetables.
4. Cook on low for 6 hours until vegetables are tender.
5. Serve the tagine over cooked rice.

Nutritional Facts: (Per serving)

- ❖ Calories: 280
- ❖ Protein: 6g
- ❖ Carbohydrates: 55g
- ❖ Fat: 3g
- ❖ Fiber: 8g
- ❖ Sodium: 300mg

Conclude your day with this Moroccan Tagine, a dish that brings a piece of Morocco to your table. It's a perfect blend of spices and vegetables, offering a healthy and exotic meal that's as enjoyable to cook as it is.

Recipe 30: Pumpkin Lentil Curry and Rice

Embark on a culinary adventure with Pumpkin Lentil Curry and Rice, a slow cooker dish that melds the sweetness of pumpkin with the earthiness of lentils in a flavorful curry. This vegetarian recipe for two is a testament to simplicity and taste, providing a warm, nourishing meal perfect for cozy evenings or any day that calls for a touch of spice.

Servings: 2

Prepping Time: 15 minutes

Cook Time: 6 hours

Difficulty: Easy

Ingredients:

- ✓ 1 cup pumpkin, cubed
- ✓ 1/2 cup red lentils
- ✓ 1 onion, chopped
- ✓ 2 cloves garlic, minced
- ✓ 1 tbsp curry powder
- ✓ 1 tsp cumin
- ✓ 2 cups vegetable broth
- ✓ Salt and pepper, to taste
- ✓ 1 cup cooked rice for serving

Step-by-Step Preparation:

1. Place pumpkin, red lentils, onion, and garlic in the slow cooker.
2. Sprinkle with curry powder, cumin, salt, and pepper.
3. Pour vegetable broth over the mixture.
4. Cook on low for 6 hours until the pumpkin and lentils are tender.
5. Serve the curry over cooked rice.

Nutritional Facts: (Per serving)

- ❖ Calories: 350
- ❖ Protein: 14g
- ❖ Carbohydrates: 65g
- ❖ Fat: 3g
- ❖ Fiber: 15g
- ❖ Sodium: 300mg

End your day with this comforting Pumpkin Lentil Curry and Rice, a dish that's as nourishing as it is flavorful. It's a beautiful way to enjoy the depth of curry spices balanced with the natural sweetness of pumpkin, making for a satisfying vegetarian meal.

Chapter 04: Fish & Seafood Treats

Recipe 31: Slow Cooker Salmon Risotto

Experience the luxury of Slow Cooker Salmon Risotto, a dish that combines the rich flavors of salmon with creamy risotto, all prepared conveniently from a slow cooker. This recipe serves two, offering a sophisticated yet effortless meal perfect for a special evening or when you want to indulge in a sumptuous seafood delight.

Servings: 2

Prepping Time: 10 minutes

Cook Time: 2 hours

Difficulty: Medium

Ingredients:

- ✓ 2 salmon fillets
- ✓ 1 cup Arborio rice
- ✓ 1 onion, finely chopped
- ✓ 2 cloves garlic, minced
- ✓ 3 cups chicken or vegetable broth
- ✓ 1/2 cup white wine
- ✓ 1 tbsp olive oil
- ✓ Salt and pepper, to taste
- ✓ Fresh parsley for garnish
- ✓ Grated Parmesan cheese for serving

Step-by-Step Preparation:

1. Heat olive oil in a pan and sauté onion and garlic until soft.
2. Add Arborio rice, stirring to coat with oil.
3. Transfer the rice mixture to the slow cooker.
4. Pour in broth and white wine. Season with salt and pepper.
5. Place salmon fillets on top of the rice.
6. Cook on low for 2 hours until rice is creamy and salmon is cooked.
7. Flake the salmon into the risotto gently.
8. Serve garnished with parsley and grated Parmesan cheese.

Nutritional Facts: (Per serving)

- ❖ Calories: 560
- ❖ Protein: 35g
- ❖ Carbohydrates: 65g
- ❖ Fat: 15g
- ❖ Fiber: 2g
- ❖ Sodium: 300mg

This Slow Cooker Salmon Risotto is a harmonious blend of simplicity and elegance, making it an ideal dish for those seeking a gourmet experience at home. Enjoy the luxurious taste of salmon and the creamy texture of risotto, a perfect meal to impress or savor.

Recipe 32: Tuna Noodles Fish Soup

Dive into the comforting flavors of Tuna Noodles and ish Soup, a delightful slow cooker dish that brings the best of the sea to your table. Perfect for two, this recipe offers a delicious blend of tender tuna and hearty noodles in a savory broth, making it an ideal choice for a simple yet satisfying seafood meal.

Servings: 2

Cook Time: 4 hours

Prepping Time: 15 minutes

Difficulty: Easy

Ingredients:

- ✓ 2 tuna steaks
- ✓ 1 cup egg noodles
- ✓ 1 onion, chopped
- ✓ 2 cloves garlic, minced
- ✓ 1 carrot, sliced
- ✓ 2 cups fish or vegetable broth
- ✓ 1 tsp dried dill
- ✓ Salt and pepper, to taste

Step-by-Step Preparation:

1. Place tuna steaks, onion, garlic, and carrot in the slow cooker.
2. Season with dill, salt, and pepper.
3. Pour broth over the ingredients.
4. Cook on low for 3 hours.
5. Add egg noodles and cook for an additional hour until noodles are tender.
6. Flake the tuna into smaller pieces and stir gently before serving.

Nutritional Facts: (Per serving)

- ❖ Calories: 380
- ❖ Protein: 40g
- ❖ Carbohydrates: 35g
- ❖ Fat: 10g
- ❖ Fiber: 3g
- ❖ Sodium: 500mg

Conclude your day with this warming Tuna Noodles Fish Soup, a dish that combines the heartiness of noodles with the lightness of tuna, creating a perfectly balanced meal. It's an easy and delightful way to enjoy seafood, ideal for those who love the flavors of the ocean.

Recipe 33: Fish Broth or Stock of Salmon

Discover the essence of flavor with this homemade fish broth or stock, crafted from the rich and savory notes of salmon. A fundamental recipe for any seafood lover, this slow cooker fish broth is perfect for two, offering a base for countless dishes or a comforting drink steeped in health benefits and exquisite taste.

Servings: 2

Prepping Time: 10 minutes

Cook Time: 8 hours

Difficulty: Easy

Ingredients:

- ✓ Bones and skin of 1 salmon
- ✓ 1 onion, quartered
- ✓ 2 carrots, chopped
- ✓ 2 celery stalks, chopped
- ✓ 1 bay leaf
- ✓ 6 cups water
- ✓ Salt and pepper, to taste

Step-by-Step Preparation:

1. Place salmon bones, skin, onion, carrots, celery, and bay leaf in the slow cooker.
2. Fill with water until the ingredients are fully covered.
3. Season with salt and pepper.
4. Cook on low for 8 hours, allowing flavors to infuse.
5. Strain the broth, discarding solids.

Nutritional Facts: (Per serving)

- ❖ Calories: 50
- ❖ Protein: 5g
- ❖ Carbohydrates: 5g
- ❖ Fat: 0g
- ❖ Fiber: 1g
- ❖ Sodium: 100mg

Enjoy this rich and nourishing fish broth or stock, a culinary treasure that's as versatile as it is delicious. Use it as a base for soups and stews, or savor it on its own for a warm, healthful drink, embodying the deep flavors of the sea.

Recipe 34: Fish Stew, Ukha, Fish Soup

Embark on a culinary voyage with Ukha, the classic Russian fish stew reimagined in your slow cooker. This heartwarming fish soup, perfect for two, combines fresh fish with aromatic herbs and vegetables, creating a light yet flavorful broth that's both comforting and nourishing, ideal for a cozy evening or a wholesome lunch.

Servings: 2

Prepping Time: 20 minutes

Cook Time: 4 hours

Difficulty: Easy

Ingredients:

- ✓ 2 fish fillets (such as salmon or cod)
- ✓ 4 cups water
- ✓ 1 onion, chopped
- ✓ 2 potatoes, cubed
- ✓ 1 carrot, sliced
- ✓ 1 bay leaf
- ✓ 1 tsp dill, chopped
- ✓ Salt and pepper, to taste

Step-by-Step Preparation:

1. Place fish fillets, onion, potatoes, and carrots in the slow cooker.
2. Add water, ensuring all ingredients are submerged.
3. Season with bay leaf, dill, salt, and pepper.
4. Cook on low for 4 hours, until vegetables are tender and fish is cooked.
5. Break the fish into bite-sized pieces and stir gently before serving.

Nutritional Facts: (Per serving)

- ❖ Calories: 220
- ❖ Protein: 25g
- ❖ Carbohydrates: 20g
- ❖ Fat: 5g
- ❖ Fiber: 3g
- ❖ Sodium: 70mg

Conclude your day with this soothing Ukha, a dish that brings the simple pleasures of a traditional fish stew to your table. Its delicate flavors and easy preparation make it an excellent choice for a nutritious and satisfying meal.

Recipe 35: Paella With Shrimps and Mussels

Embark on a gastronomic journey to Spain with this Paella with shrimp and Mussels, crafted to perfection in your slow cooker. Ideal for seafood enthusiasts, this dish for two captures the essence of traditional Spanish cuisine, blending the ocean's bounty with aromatic spices and rice, creating a feast that's as visually appealing as it is delicious.

Servings: 2

Prepping Time: 30 minutes

Cook Time: 3 hours

Difficulty: Medium

Ingredients:

- ✓ 1 cup paella rice
- ✓ 200g shrimps, peeled and deveined
- ✓ 200g mussels, cleaned
- ✓ 1 onion, chopped
- ✓ 1 bell pepper, sliced
- ✓ 2 cloves garlic, minced
- ✓ 1/2 cup peas
- ✓ 2 cups fish or chicken broth
- ✓ 1 tsp paprika
- ✓ 1 pinch saffron
- ✓ Salt and pepper, to taste
- ✓ 2 tbsp olive oil
- ✓ Lemon wedges for serving

Step-by-Step Preparation:

1. Sauté onion, bell pepper, and garlic in olive oil until softened. Transfer to the slow cooker.
2. Add paella rice, shrimp, mussels, and peas to the cooker.
3. Season with paprika, saffron, salt, and pepper.
4. Pour broth over the mixture.
5. Cook on low for 3 hours until tender rice and seafood are cooked.
6. Serve with lemon wedges for added zest.

Nutritional Facts: (Per serving)

- ❖ Calories: 520
- ❖ Protein: 40g
- ❖ Carbohydrates: 65g
- ❖ Fat: 15g
- ❖ Fiber: 4g
- ❖ Sodium: 700mg

Conclude your day with this exquisite Paella with Shrimp and Mussels, a dish that brings Spain's vibrant flavors and colors to your table. It's a perfect blend of simplicity and luxury, ideal for a special night or a celebration of fine cuisine.

Recipe 36: Stew of Bacalao (Dried Cod) Confit

Indulge in a culinary delight with this exquisite stew of Bacalao, where dried cod is masterfully confit in extra virgin olive oil. This slow cooker dish for two is a nod to traditional flavors, offering a rich and tender fish experience. It's a simple yet sophisticated meal, perfect for those seeking to explore the depths of seafood cuisine.

Servings: 2

Prepping Time: 24 hours (for soaking Bacalao)

Cook Time: 3 hours

Difficulty: Medium

Ingredients:

- ✓ 2 Bacalao (dried cod) fillets, soaked and desalted
- ✓ 1 cup extra virgin olive oil
- ✓ 2 garlic cloves, sliced
- ✓ 1 onion, thinly sliced
- ✓ 1 bay leaf
- ✓ Salt and pepper, to taste

Step-by-Step Preparation:

1. Soak the Bacalao in water for 24 hours, changing the water several times.
2. Place the desalted Bacalao in the slow cooker.
3. Cover with extra virgin olive oil.
4. Add garlic, onion, and bay leaf.
5. Cook on low for 3 hours until the fish is tender and flavors are infused.
6. Season with salt and pepper to taste.

Nutritional Facts: (Per serving)

- ❖ Calories: 560
- ❖ Protein: 38g
- ❖ Carbohydrates: 5g
- ❖ Fat: 44g
- ❖ Fiber: 1g
- ❖ Sodium: 500mg

Savor the luxurious texture and depth of flavor in this Bacalao stew, a dish that transcends the ordinary and brings a touch of gourmet to your dining experience. It's an elegant and flavorful way to enjoy a timeless seafood classic.

Recipe 37: Salmon With Spinach and Teriyaki Sauce

Experience a fusion of flavors with Salmon with Spinach and Teriyaki Sauce, a delightful slow cooker dish perfect for two. This recipe combines salmon's richness with spinach's freshness, all beautifully complemented by the sweet and savory teriyaki sauce. It's an easy yet elegant meal for those seeking a nutritious and delicious seafood experience.

Servings: 2

Cook Time: 2 hours

Prepping Time: 10 minutes

Difficulty: Easy

Ingredients:

- ✓ 2 salmon fillets
- ✓ 2 cups fresh spinach
- ✓ 1/2 cup teriyaki sauce
- ✓ 1 garlic clove, minced
- ✓ 1 tbsp sesame oil
- ✓ Salt and pepper, to taste
- ✓ Sesame seeds, for garnish

Step-by-Step Preparation:

1. Place salmon fillets in the slow cooker.
2. In a bowl, mix teriyaki sauce, garlic, and sesame oil. Pour over salmon.
3. Season with salt and pepper.
4. Cook on low for 2 hours.
5. In the last 30 minutes, add fresh spinach to the cooker.
6. Garnish with sesame seeds before serving.

Nutritional Facts: (Per serving)

- ❖ Calories: 360
- ❖ Protein: 35g
- ❖ Carbohydrates: 15g
- ❖ Fat: 18g
- ❖ Fiber: 2g
- ❖ Sodium: 900mg

Enjoy the delightful harmony of Salmon with Spinach and Teriyaki Sauce, a dish that's as pleasing to the palate as it is to the eyes. It's a perfect choice for a special dinner or when you crave a touch of gourmet in your everyday meals.

Recipe 38: Citrus Salmon With Herb Salad

Welcome a burst of fresh flavors with Citrus Salmon and Herb Salad, a delightful slow cooker dish that serves two. This recipe beautifully marries the zestiness of citrus with the rich taste of salmon, complemented by a refreshing herb salad. It's a perfect blend of health and flavor, ideal for those seeking a light yet satisfying seafood meal.

Servings: 2

Prepping Time: 15 minutes

Cook Time: 2 hours

Difficulty: Easy

Ingredients:

- ✓ 2 salmon fillets
- ✓ 1 orange, sliced
- ✓ 1 lemon, sliced
- ✓ 1 cup mixed herbs (parsley, dill, cilantro)
- ✓ 2 tbsp olive oil
- ✓ Salt and pepper, to taste
- ✓ Lemon juice for dressing

Step-by-Step Preparation:

1. Place salmon fillets in the slow cooker.
2. Top with slices of orange and lemon.
3. Season with salt and pepper.
4. Cook on low for 2 hours until salmon is tender.
5. Mix herbs with olive oil and lemon juice to create the salad.
6. Serve salmon with a fresh herb salad.

Nutritional Facts: (Per serving)

- ❖ Calories: 340
- ❖ Protein: 25g
- ❖ Carbohydrates: 10g
- ❖ Fat: 22g
- ❖ Fiber: 3g
- ❖ Sodium: 70mg

Conclude your day with this exquisite Citrus Salmon and Herb Salad, a dish that combines the tang of citrus and the freshness of herbs to create a dining experience that's both rejuvenating and indulgent. It's perfect for a light, healthy, and flavorful meal.

Recipe 39: Salmon Fillet Steak With Salad

Indulge in Sous-Vide Cooking Salmon Fish's exquisite taste and texture, a slow-cooked salmon fillet steak that promises a culinary delight. This method ensures perfectly cooked salmon, paired with a fresh salad, making for a sophisticated and healthy meal for two. It's an ideal choice for those who appreciate the finer nuances of seafood preparation.

Servings: 2

Cook Time: 1 hour

Prepping Time: 10 minutes

Difficulty: Medium

Ingredients:

- ✓ 2 salmon fillet steaks
- ✓ 1 tbsp olive oil
- ✓ Salt and pepper, to taste
- ✓ Salad greens for serving

Step-by-Step Preparation:

1. Season salmon fillets with salt and pepper.
2. Place each fillet in a vacuum-sealed bag with olive oil.
3. Cook in a slow cooker filled with water at a controlled temperature for 1 hour.
4. Remove the salmon carefully from the bag.
5. Serve the salmon with a side of fresh salad greens.

Nutritional Facts: (Per serving)

- ❖ Calories: 280
- ❖ Fat: 20g
- ❖ Protein: 23g
- ❖ Fiber: 0g
- ❖ Carbohydrates: 0g
- ❖ Sodium: 75mg

Experience the delicate, melt-in-your-mouth texture of this Sous-Vide Cooked Salmon, a dish that elevates the simple salmon steak to a gourmet level. Paired with a light salad, it's the perfect combination of health and flavor, ideal for a special occasion or a refined dinner for two.

Recipe 40: Slow Cooked Octopus

Embark on a gastronomic adventure with this exquisite slow-cooked octopus dish, complemented by creamy avocado purée, dehydrated tomatoes, vibrant pesto, and cooked cherry tomatoes. Perfect for seafood lovers, this recipe for two is a symphony of flavors and textures, blending the tenderness of octopus with a medley of fresh and rich accompaniments for a truly gourmet experience.

Servings: 2

Cook Time: 4 hours

Prepping Time: 30 minutes

Difficulty: Medium

Ingredients:

- ✓ 1 small octopus, cleaned
- ✓ 1 avocado
- ✓ 1/2 cup cherry tomatoes
- ✓ 1/4 cup dehydrated tomatoes
- ✓ 2 tbsp pesto sauce
- ✓ Salt and pepper, to taste
- ✓ Olive oil for cooking

Step-by-Step Preparation:

1. Place the octopus in the slow cooker with a bit of olive oil. Cook on low for 4 hours until tender.
2. Blend avocado with a pinch of salt to make the puree.
3. Cook cherry tomatoes in a pan until soft.
4. Arrange the cooked octopus on a plate with avocado puree, dehydrated tomatoes, and cooked cherry tomatoes.
5. Drizzle with pesto sauce before serving.

Nutritional Facts: (Per serving)

- ❖ Calories: 350
- ❖ Protein: 25g
- ❖ Carbohydrates: 20g
- ❖ Fat: 20g
- ❖ Fiber: 7g
- ❖ Sodium: 700mg

Conclude your culinary journey with this Slow Cooked Octopus, a dish that pleases the palate and the eyes. It's a perfect blend of the ocean's bounty and the earth's produce, creating a dining experience that's both luxurious and satisfying.

Chapter 05: Bite-Sized Snack Temptations

Recipe 41: Pumpkin Soup Puree With Seeds

Immerse yourself in the comforting embrace of Pumpkin Soup Purée, a slow cooker delight infused with the richness of coconut cream and the earthy touch of thyme. Topped with crunchy seeds, this soup for two is a warm, velvety indulgence, perfect for cozy evenings or as a nourishing start to any meal.

Servings: 2

Cook Time: 6 hours

Prepping Time: 15 minutes

Difficulty: Easy

Ingredients:

- ✓ 2 cups pumpkin, cubed
- ✓ 1 onion, chopped
- ✓ 2 cloves garlic, minced
- ✓ 2 cups vegetable broth
- ✓ 1/2 cup coconut cream
- ✓ 1 tsp dried thyme
- ✓ Salt and pepper, to taste
- ✓ Pumpkin seeds, for garnish

Step-by-Step Preparation:

1. Place pumpkin, onion, and garlic in the slow cooker.
2. Pour in vegetable broth. Season with thyme, salt, and pepper.
3. Cook on low for 6 hours until pumpkin is soft.
4. Blend the mixture into a smooth purée.
5. Stir in coconut cream.
6. Serve hot, garnished with pumpkin seeds.

Nutritional Facts: (Per serving)

- ❖ Calories: 220
- ❖ Protein: 3g
- ❖ Carbohydrates: 25g
- ❖ Fat: 12g
- ❖ Fiber: 5g
- ❖ Sodium: 500mg

Relish the simple yet profound flavors of this Pumpkin Soup Purée, a dish that's as soothing as it is flavorful. It's an ideal way to enjoy the essence of autumn, bringing warmth and comfort to your dining experience.

Recipe 42: Fish Broth or Soup of Salmon

Delve into the soothing world of homemade fish broth, a slow cooker soup crafted from salmon, aromatic vegetables, and a blend of herbs and spices. Perfect for two, this broth offers a rich depth of flavor and embodies the essence of nourishing simplicity, ideal for a comforting meal or a flavorful base for other culinary creations.

Servings: 2

Cook Time: 4 hours

Prepping Time: 15 minutes

Difficulty: Easy

Ingredients:

- ✓ 2 salmon fillets
- ✓ 1 onion, chopped
- ✓ 1 carrot, chopped
- ✓ 1 celery stalk, chopped
- ✓ 1 bay leaf
- ✓ 1 tsp dried thyme
- ✓ Salt and pepper, to taste
- ✓ 4 cups water

Step-by-Step Preparation:

1. Place salmon fillets in the slow cooker.
2. Add onion, carrot, celery, bay leaf, and thyme.
3. Season with salt and pepper.
4. Pour water over the ingredients.
5. Cook on low for 4 hours.
6. Strain the soup, discarding solids.

Nutritional Facts: (Per serving)

- ❖ Calories: 120
- ❖ Protein: 20g
- ❖ Carbohydrates: 5g
- ❖ Fat: 3g
- ❖ Fiber: 1g
- ❖ Sodium: 70mg

Savor the delicate flavors of this fish broth, a testament to the power of simple ingredients coming together to create a soothing and satisfying soup. It's ideal for a light yet flavorful meal or as a base for more elaborate seafood dishes.

Recipe 43: White Bean Soup

Delight in the hearty and comforting flavors of White Bean Soup, a perfect slow cooker dish for two. This soup blends the richness of beans with the savory taste of ham and the sweetness of carrots; all garnished with fresh parsley. It's an ideal recipe for those seeking a warm, filling, nutritious meal, especially on chilly days.

Servings: 2

Prepping Time: 15 minutes

Cook Time: 8 hours

Difficulty: Easy

Ingredients:

- ✓ 1 cup white beans, soaked overnight
- ✓ 1 carrot, chopped
- ✓ 100g ham, diced
- ✓ 1 onion, chopped
- ✓ 2 cloves garlic, minced
- ✓ 4 cups chicken or vegetable broth
- ✓ Salt and pepper, to taste
- ✓ Fresh parsley for garnish

Step-by-Step Preparation:

1. Drain and rinse the soaked beans.
2. Place beans, carrots, ham, onion, and garlic in the slow cooker.
3. Add broth. Season with salt and pepper.
4. Cook on low for 8 hours until beans are tender.
5. Adjust seasoning if necessary.
6. Garnish with fresh parsley before serving.

Nutritional Facts: (Per serving)

- ❖ Calories: 320
- ❖ Protein: 20g
- ❖ Carbohydrates: 45g
- ❖ Fat: 8g
- ❖ Fiber: 10g
- ❖ Sodium: 950mg

End your day with this comforting White Bean Soup, a simple yet satisfying dish that brings warmth and wholesomeness to your table. It's a perfect blend of flavors and textures, ideal for those cozy nights.

Recipe 44: Mushroom Soup

Savor the earthy and comforting essence of Mushroom Soup, a slow cooker delight perfect for two. This recipe brings out the rich, umami flavors of mushrooms in a creamy, soothing broth. It's an ideal dish for mushroom lovers and those seeking a warm, inviting meal that's both simple to prepare and deeply satisfying.

Servings: 2

Cook Time: 6 hours

Prepping Time: 15 minutes

Difficulty: Easy

Ingredients:

- ✓ 2 cups mushrooms, sliced
- ✓ 1 onion, chopped
- ✓ 2 cloves garlic, minced
- ✓ 2 cups vegetable broth
- ✓ 1 cup heavy cream
- ✓ Salt and pepper, to taste
- ✓ Fresh parsley for garnish

Step-by-Step Preparation:

1. Place mushrooms, onion, and garlic in the slow cooker.
2. Pour vegetable broth over the ingredients.
3. Cook on low for 6 hours until mushrooms are tender.
4. Blend the soup to the desired consistency.
5. Stir in heavy cream.
6. Season with salt and pepper.
7. Garnish with fresh parsley before serving.

Nutritional Facts: (Per serving)

- ❖ Calories: 280
- ❖ Protein: 4g
- ❖ Carbohydrates: 15g
- ❖ Fat: 24g
- ❖ Fiber: 2g
- ❖ Sodium: 500mg

Conclude your day with this luxurious Mushroom Soup, a dish that promises a delicious and hearty experience. It's perfect for those evenings when you need comfort, offering a blend of rich flavors and creamy texture that's sure to delight.

Recipe 45: Lasagna Soup

Indulge in the innovative twist of Lasagna Soup, an Italian-inspired creation that combines the rich flavors of tomato soup with the heartiness of pasta. Perfect for two, this slow cooker dish is a delightful amalgamation of classic lasagna elements in a comforting soup form, making it an ideal choice for those craving Italian flavors in a unique, easy-to-prepare meal.

Servings: 2

Prepping Time: 15 minutes

Cook Time: 6 hours

Difficulty: Easy

Ingredients:

- ✓ 2 cups crushed tomatoes
- ✓ 2 cups vegetable broth
- ✓ 1/2 cup lasagna pasta, broken into pieces
- ✓ 1 onion, chopped
- ✓ 2 cloves garlic, minced
- ✓ 1 tsp Italian seasoning
- ✓ Salt and pepper, to taste
- ✓ Grated Parmesan cheese for serving
- ✓ Fresh basil for garnish

Step-by-Step Preparation:

1. Place crushed tomatoes, vegetable broth, onion, and garlic in the slow cooker.
2. Season with Italian seasoning, salt, and pepper.
3. Cook on low for 6 hours.
4. In the last 30 minutes, add the lasagna pasta pieces.
5. Serve hot, topped with grated Parmesan cheese and fresh basil.

Nutritional Facts: (Per serving)

- ❖ Calories: 220
- ❖ Protein: 8g
- ❖ Carbohydrates: 40g
- ❖ Fat: 4g
- ❖ Fiber: 6g
- ❖ Sodium: 700mg

Finish your day with this comforting bowl of Lasagna Soup, a creative and delightful dish that brings the essence of Italian cuisine to your table in a novel way. It's a perfect choice for a cozy, flavorful meal that combines the joy of soup with the love of pasta.

Recipe 46: Lentil Soup With Potatoes and Carrots

Embark on a journey of comfort and nourishment with Lentil Soup, a slow cooker delight featuring potatoes and carrots. This wholesome recipe, perfect for two, is a symphony of hearty lentils, earthy potatoes, and sweet carrots, all simmered to perfection. It's ideal for those seeking a healthy, comforting, and easy-to-make meal.

Servings: 2

Cook Time: 8 hours

Prepping Time: 15 minutes

Difficulty: Easy

Ingredients:

- ✓ 1 cup lentils, rinsed
- ✓ 1 large potato, cubed
- ✓ 2 carrots, sliced
- ✓ 1 onion, chopped
- ✓ 2 cloves garlic, minced
- ✓ 4 cups vegetable broth
- ✓ 1 tsp cumin
- ✓ Salt and pepper, to taste

Step-by-Step Preparation:

1. Place lentils, potato, carrots, onion, and garlic in the slow cooker.
2. Add vegetable broth. Season with cumin, salt, and pepper.
3. Cook on low for 8 hours until lentils and vegetables are tender.
4. Adjust seasoning if needed before serving.

Nutritional Facts: (Per serving)

- ❖ Calories: 320
- ❖ Protein: 18g
- ❖ Carbohydrates: 60g
- ❖ Fat: 2g
- ❖ Fiber: 15g
- ❖ Sodium: 300mg

Enjoy the heartiness of this Lentil Soup with Potatoes and Carrots, a dish that brings warmth and nutrition to your table. It's a perfect blend of simplicity and flavor, ideal for a cozy night or a healthy, fulfilling lunch.

Recipe 47: Beef Meat Slow-Cooked Soup

Immerse yourself in the rich and hearty flavors of a slow-cooked Beef Meat Soup, a nourishing dish perfect for two. This soup combines tender beef with a medley of vegetables like carrots, potatoes, corn, and sweet potatoes, creating a comforting and satisfying meal—ideal for those chilly days or when you crave a taste of home-style cooking.

Servings: 2

Prepping Time: 20 minutes

Cook Time: 8 hours

Difficulty: Easy

Ingredients:

- ✓ 300g beef, cubed
- ✓ 1 carrot, sliced
- ✓ 1 potato, cubed
- ✓ 1 sweet potato, cubed
- ✓ 1/2 cup corn kernels
- ✓ 4 cups beef broth
- ✓ Salt and pepper, to taste
- ✓ Fresh herbs (parsley or thyme) for garnish

Step-by-Step Preparation:

1. Place beef cubes in the slow cooker.
2. Add carrot, potato, sweet potato, and corn.
3. Pour beef broth over the ingredients. Season with salt and pepper.
4. Cook on low for 8 hours until the beef is tender and vegetables are cooked.
5. Garnish with fresh herbs before serving.

Nutritional Facts: (Per serving)

- ❖ Calories: 480
- ❖ Protein: 35g
- ❖ Carbohydrates: 55g
- ❖ Fat: 15g
- ❖ Fiber: 8g
- ❖ Sodium: 800mg

Conclude your day with this soul-warming Beef Meat Soup, a dish that satisfies your hunger and comforts your heart. It's a perfect blend of rich flavors and wholesome ingredients, ideal for a relaxing evening or a nourishing meal anytime.

Recipe 48: Chicken Noodle Soup

Soothe your soul with the classic comfort of Chicken Noodle Soup, a slow cooker dish perfect for two. This timeless recipe combines tender chicken, nourishing noodles, and a blend of vegetables simmered to create a warm, comforting broth. It's the ideal remedy for a cold day or when you need a touch of home-cooked goodness.

Servings: 2

Cook Time: 6 hours

Prepping Time: 15 minutes

Difficulty: Easy

Ingredients:

- ✓ 2 chicken breasts
- ✓ 1 carrot, sliced
- ✓ 1 celery stalk, chopped
- ✓ 1 onion, chopped
- ✓ 4 cups chicken broth
- ✓ 1 cup egg noodles
- ✓ Salt and pepper, to taste
- ✓ Fresh parsley for garnish

Step-by-Step Preparation:

1. Place chicken breasts in the slow cooker.
2. Add carrot, celery, and onion.
3. Pour chicken broth over the ingredients. Season with salt and pepper.
4. Cook on low for 6 hours until chicken is tender.
5. Shred the chicken and return to the soup.
6. Add egg noodles and cook for an additional 20 minutes.
7. Garnish with fresh parsley before serving.

Nutritional Facts: (Per serving)

- ❖ Calories: 300
- ❖ Protein: 25g
- ❖ Carbohydrates: 30g
- ❖ Fat: 8g
- ❖ Fiber: 3g
- ❖ Sodium: 800mg

End your day with this heartwarming bowl of Chicken Noodle Soup, a simple yet fulfilling dish that brings comfort with every spoonful. It's a perfect blend of wholesome ingredients and tender care, ideal for those moments when you need a warm embrace in a meal.

Recipe 49: Vegetable Soup

Dive into the wholesome world of Vegetable Soup, a delightful slow cooker dish that serves two. This soup is a vibrant mix of fresh vegetables, simmered to perfection, offering a nutritious and comforting meal. For those seeking a healthy, easy-to-make dish, it's perfect for a light lunch or warming dinner on a fantastic evening.

Servings: 2

Prepping Time: 15 minutes

Cook Time: 6 hours

Difficulty: Easy

Ingredients:

- ✓ 1 carrot, chopped
- ✓ 1 potato, cubed
- ✓ 1 onion, chopped
- ✓ 1 celery stalk, chopped
- ✓ 1 cup green beans, trimmed
- ✓ 4 cups vegetable broth
- ✓ 1 tsp dried basil
- ✓ Salt and pepper, to taste

Step-by-Step Preparation:

1. Place all chopped vegetables in the slow cooker.
2. Add vegetable broth and season with dried basil, salt, and pepper.
3. Cook on low for 6 hours until vegetables are tender.
4. Adjust seasoning as needed before serving.

Nutritional Facts: (Per serving)

- ❖ Calories: 150
- ❖ Protein: 4g
- ❖ Carbohydrates: 30g
- ❖ Fat: 1g
- ❖ Fiber: 6g
- ❖ Sodium: 480mg

Conclude your day with this nourishing bowl of Vegetable Soup, a dish that's as satisfying as it is healthy. It's a perfect way to enjoy a variety of vegetables in one meal, providing both comfort and nutrition in every spoonful.

Recipe 50: Slow Cooker Chicken Taco Soup

Embark on a flavorful journey with Slow Cooker Chicken Taco Soup, a dish that effortlessly combines the zest of tacos with the comfort of soup. This recipe for two is topped with fresh cilantro and avocado and brings a Mexican flair to your dinner table. It's perfect for those seeking a hearty, easy-to-make meal with a twist of freshness.

Servings: 2

Prepping Time: 15 minutes

Cook Time: 6 hours

Difficulty: Easy

Ingredients:

- ✓ 2 chicken breasts
- ✓ 1 can diced tomatoes
- ✓ 1 can black beans, drained
- ✓ 1 cup corn
- ✓ 1 onion, chopped
- ✓ 2 cloves garlic, minced
- ✓ 1 tbsp taco seasoning
- ✓ 2 cups chicken broth
- ✓ Fresh cilantro for garnish
- ✓ 1 avocado, sliced, for garnish

Step-by-Step Preparation:

1. Place chicken breasts in the slow cooker.
2. Add diced tomatoes, black beans, corn, onion, and garlic.
3. Sprinkle with taco seasoning.
4. Pour chicken broth over the mixture.
5. Cook on low for 6 hours until chicken is tender.
6. Shred the chicken and return to the soup.
7. Serve topped with fresh cilantro and avocado slices.

Nutritional Facts: (Per serving)

- ❖ Calories: 360
- ❖ Protein: 30g
- ❖ Carbohydrates: 40g
- ❖ Fat: 12g
- ❖ Fiber: 10g
- ❖ Sodium: 700mg

Enjoy this delightful Chicken Taco Soup blend of robust flavors and freshness. It's a comforting and nutritious dish that brings a creative spin to your regular soup routine, ideal for a cozy night in or a casual dining experience.

Conclusion

As we come to the close of "Slow Cooker Success: Cookbook with Easy Instructions for Two," it's time to reflect on the culinary journey we've embarked upon together. David Clark has expertly guided us through the simplicity and elegance of slow cooking, presenting a collection that celebrates the joy of shared meals, the artistry of cooking, and the beauty of authentic recipes. This cookbook is not merely a collection of recipes; it's an invitation to explore the depths of flavor, embrace the ease of slow cooking, and enjoy creating nourishing meals for two.

We began this journey with anticipation, eager to discover the flavorful possibilities within each chapter. Every recipe has been a revelation, from the hearty meats to the delicate fish and seafood, from the robust vegetarian dishes to the comforting soups. David Clark has ensured that every meal is an opportunity for connection, a moment to savor the food and the company with which it's shared.

"Slow Cooker Success" has brought the versatility of slow cooking to the forefront, demonstrating that with the proper instructions, even the most complex flavors can be easily achieved. The book's structure, divided into five comprehensive chapters, has provided a roadmap for cooks of all levels to navigate the rich terrain of slow-cooked cuisine confidently.

Each recipe, accompanied by vivid, original photography, has transformed cooking into an immersive experience. These images have served as a visual guide and inspired us to strive for those perfect tests and flavors, ensuring that what we bring to the table is nothing short of spectacular.

As we conclude our journey, let's carry forward the lessons learned and the flavors discovered. "Slow Cooker Success" has equipped us with the tools and knowledge to continue exploring the possibilities of slow cooking, inviting us to make each meal an occasion. Whether you're a seasoned chef or a beginner, the essence of this cookbook is to inspire continued culinary exploration, encourage shared experiences, and foster a love for cooking that transcends the pages.

David Clark's commitment to quality, evident in the meticulous attention to detail and the absence of grammatical or spelling errors, has ensured that "Slow Cooker Success: Cookbook with Easy Instructions for Two" is not just a guide but a companion in your cooking journey. As we part ways with this book, remember that the journey of cooking and sharing meals is an endless adventure, one that is continually enriched with each dish you prepare.

Made in the USA
Monee, IL
06 December 2024